Auschwitz Trials:

letters from an eyewitness

Auschwitz Trials

letters from an eyewitness

BY EMMI BONHOEFFER

TRANSLATED BY URSULA STECHOW

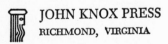 JOHN KNOX PRESS
RICHMOND, VIRGINIA

102086

Translated from the German edition, *Zeugen im Auschwitz-Prozess,* published by Johannes Kiefel Verlag.

LIBRARY OF CONGRESS CATALOG NUMBER: 67-22001
© M. E. BRATCHER 1967
PRINTED IN THE UNITED STATES OF AMERICA
J. 4365(20)1727

*These letters are addressed
to Mrs. Recha Jaszi in Oberlin, Ohio,
to whom I have been indebted
ever since my husband's death for
the warmest understanding, the most
helpful trust, and ever vital stimulation
and encouragement.*

February, 1965
E. B.

PREFACE

Any report about these trials, which even though the largest and longest of them all are but one series in many held these years, must stir our heart, our conscience, and our memory. And any report should serve as an attempt to penetrate the wall that has kept us so safely away from all this horror, to make this wall less thick, even to break it down, so that we might learn to be ready to live eye to eye with what has happened and no longer hide—be it in cowardice, insensitivity, or self-conceit—from what, after all, was part of our own past and thus of our own lives. We may not want to admit that it was, for it is not easy to let it be true.

The papers say that opinion polls report the majority of our people to be against these trials—largely the same majority that would favor capital punishment for murderers of taxi drivers, and thus quite likely the same people who would let one category of crime go unpunished while wishing severest sentences for others.

Among the reasons against the trials, as quoted by Emmi Bonhoeffer, the most weighty seems to me the one least often stated: punishment asked for the murderer of a taxi driver is not something which threatens us ourselves; compared to him, we are the innocent, the just. But with the atrocities of the Hitler regime, with the gruesome murder of Jews, Gypsies, Poles, Russians, Communists, etc., we are in some way linked. Most of us have at one time or another seen some promise in Hitler's plans; have perhaps ourselves looked down upon the groups he set out to destroy; have looked on or turned away when the atrocities began; have kept the knowledge and the thought of them out of our mind; have, in failing to protest or to help, profited by the fact that we ourselves were not among the persecuted groups; and many of us, if not actively taking part, have had relatives or friends in the service of the Hitler movement, which has now come to be so horribly unmasked.

Therefore, innumerable people feel subconscious apprehension: if everything that happened at that time is still to come to light we may all be linked in many ways to those accused here; the question of guilt, as it is raised in these trials, will reach into our own lives as well. That is why people object to the trials; that

8

is why they want them ended. For their own sake, for the peace of their own conscience, many wish, as they say, that "the curtain finally be dropped."

It is to be hoped, however, that a report such as this one by Mrs. Bonhoeffer might show to many that it is necessary, and indeed good and wholesome, that the wish for that dropped curtain not be fulfilled. Only if we are not easy on ourselves, only if we, each one of us, take ourselves to task, only if we look back upon the past with open eyes, will we find the right path toward a future where repetition of such a past is barred and bolted out. And only then can we make full use of the opportunity the present holds for us.

The work done by these women who tended the witnesses at the Auschwitz trials in Frankfurt is an example of such opportunity. For if those who were murdered at Auschwitz are part of our past, then these witnesses and the survivors and families they represent are part of our present. Never again must they be witnesses to our insensitivity, to our indifference; today they ought to experience a little of what we neglected to show them at that time.

Therefore, we have every reason to thank Emmi Bonhoeffer, who out of her own suffering became a helper for so many, and her associates for the service which they now render on behalf of us all. From their example, may we gain awareness of opportunity wrought by the present. For not only in Frankfurt can we find witnesses and bereaved survivors of that hell, the world of the concentration camps; similar trials are being held in many other places. And by no means only at such trials do we have witnesses within our reach.

Helmut Gollwitzer

Dear Recha,

You asked what I have been doing since I laid down the work that had filled my days for twelve long years. Actually, I had decided to put in a sabbatical year: for once to live merely for children and grandchildren, for books and guests, like other women of my age. But after only twelve days of that, a phone call came from my friend Ursula Wirth in Kronberg: would I come to see her, if at all possible on that very day; she had hit upon an idea she would like to talk over with me and for which she would need my help.

11

Reading *Die Welt,* she had seen an article pointing out that while other foreign guests were being met at the airport, ushered to their hotels, and catered to with all kinds of ado, and while everyone sought to make their stay in Germany an interesting and pleasant one throughout, no one was paying the least attention to those who were arriving, summoned from all over the world, and especially from Poland, to testify as witnesses in the Auschwitz trials now being held before the grand jury in Frankfurt.

Up to this time, it seems, it had not occurred to anyone to consider what it must mean to these people twenty years after their horrible ordeal, perhaps by now at long last overcome to some extent, so suddenly to have to unearth it all once more, recall it to the last detail, and afterward have to be alone with it, alone here in this country that they had known at its worst.

At once we agreed that something needed to be done, and the very next day I listened in on a hearing of the Auschwitz trials so that I might come a little closer to the facts, as they stood then, and to the atmosphere in which these people whom we were setting out to help had to serve as witnesses.

To be quite honest: up to this time, I myself had read the reports about these trials only occasionally and with fleeting interest; perhaps I was subconsciously afraid of learning worse things than I thought I could bear. But here I was in the midst of it all, and as always in situations such as this—be they bomb attacks or Gestapo hearings—from the very moment one feels called upon to act is born the strength to bear whatever horror one will hear or see. In some inexplicable way, terror loses its overwhelming power when it becomes a task that must be faced.

My first impression of the main hearings was not only upsetting but also confusing. Of the twenty-three accused, several are at liberty: during recess they cross your path in the vestibule; they sit at the table next to yours in the canteen, or with their lawyer in the restaurant next door; successful businessmen that they are, they drive up in their Mercedes; and several of them deport themselves with an arrogance that seems to say, "Our only real mistake was that we did not kill off all the Jews."

We soon knew what overall form our work was to take, and we decided to affiliate it with the Red Cross, so as to document its nonpolitical character from the very beginning and to make it readily understandable to everyone. The Red Cross itself reacted at once and most favorably in all its echelons and gave its support to whatever we asked. Actually, to begin with, our work consisted in sitting in on the hearings three times each week, from 9-5 o'clock, with three intermissions. For if one wants to help someone, one must know before all else where his life now stands.

From now on I will report to you every week.

Dear Recha,

It is amazing how well you seem to sense the psyche of the Germans of our day, even though you have been living in the U.S.A. for forty years. It is only natural that the Auschwitz trials should be unpopular. It is that much more astounding, therefore, that the entire press nevertheless occupies itself with them every day, reporting what no one really wants to hear and what surely those will not read who need it most. As far as I can see, the inner resistance against these trials and other hearings of this kind springs from four basic roots.

15

With most people, worry naturally plays a role: Who knows what all may yet come to light! Perhaps my uncle, too . . . or even I myself . . . Quite simply, one wants to be left alone. Like birds of passage, the avenging gods were at long last disappearing over the horizon; but now an evil spirit is whirling up hot winds that drive them back once more. Why? Why all that?

The second reason for resistance to such trials seems to be that one doubts the justification for convicting these particular defendants. One feels that only under those special circumstances had they been criminals, as seems proved by the fact that never again, in the twenty years since, have they come in conflict with the law. Now I myself believe it is a basic error to see as the essential purpose of these trials the punishment that is to be meted out to a handful of people who were found out, more or less by accident, from among thousands, and against whose guilt—insofar as they are not notorious sadists—much could and surely will be said. Most important is, however, this: that a German court should document and state in public what did transpire in Auschwitz. For in this way an end could be put to the frequent and facile slighting of our wrongs; and over those who care to think, there could come a wholesome fright as they are made aware of what can happen if, tucked away somewhere in some remote corner of a country and well out of reach of a controlling public, such evil can go on for years.

The third reason for the negative attitude of most people against the so-called Nazi trials lies in their doubt whether these mass murders can be isolated for investigation apart from the total phenomenon of fascism as such. To this, I would answer that one must indeed investigate them, and not stop there, but rather feel prompted by such thorough probing to scrutinize mentally and spiritually the entire complex of problems as they pertain to the State, to its form and its rights, to the rights of man, and to consideration of his dignity.

And finally, sheer repletion with bad news, it seems to me, is one more reason for the reticence shown by so many people when they encounter news reports about the Auschwitz hearings. They feel a natural abhorrence of atrocities—a sentiment which, by the way, I understand quite well. But since I have concerned myself more closely with the whole thing, I do believe that we must face the monstrous sight. Here, too, we must not close our eyes to the reality before us.

You are right, of course: it is terrible that these trials should come about only now, twenty long years after the end of the war. However, there are many sober

17

explanations for this. Formalities play a role in it, problems of competence, difficulties in procuring proof or in searching for the criminals concerned. But inner reasons also play a role, and I consider them decisive. Any prosecution whatsoever can be put into action only after a crime has become "known"; under normal circumstances the prosecutor is informed of a criminal act by an accusation. But who likes to accuse? Especially when he is aware that the crime was somehow intertwined with a public opinion that he himself has shared. Have we not all raised our hand in the Hitler salute! One, perhaps out of conviction; another, so as not to be noticed; a third, because he thought Hitler would do away with unemployment; still another, because he, too, had felt annoyed at one time or another by some Jew; or for whatever other reason Tom, Dick, or Harry might have found to cheer this strong man who knew so wonderfully well what was to be done in the muddled situation in which the German people found themselves.

As Himmler expressed it, and as so many—by no means only the SS-men—felt or persuaded themselves to believe: "In 'solving the Jewish problem,' disagreeable though this was to the entire people, the followers of Hitler made a great sacrifice, thus doing their patriotic duty for the sake of Germany's future!" One must call all this back to mind in order to understand how much every initiative toward

prosecution was hampered by a feeling of self-guilt.

You ask why, once prosecution was begun, it still took several years for the trials to get under way. But can you not imagine the towering difficulties in collecting documents from the chaos left in the gutted administration buildings, in finding any document whatsoever after the mass displacement of streams of refugees? A special research center, in Ludwigsburg near Stuttgart, had to be established for investigation of Nazi crimes; a center which does nothing but hunt up such criminals, witnesses, and documents. What a task, when one takes into account how easy it was to hide behind an assumed name and how readily a number of countries did accept political refugees! In Cairo, even today, the hotel porter will greet you with a radiant "Heil Hitler!" if he recognizes the German in you!

The deeper the prosecution penetrated into the material, the more evident became the broad extent of the entanglement in crime that would have to be dealt with juridically. Involvement in the guilt reached all the way into the universities, which had made the false doctrine their own; into the manufacturing firms, which had made profit on the murders; into the churches, which had worshiped Hitler. Was there still any sense at all in lifting from the wide circle of those politically involved, the narrow group of those penally accountable, ever so hard to define, when the crime was thus entangled and inter-woven with an entire political fabric?

If, on the other hand, one came to be of the opinion that none but the central figures were truly punishable, then one might well say: "Questionable as the Nuremberg trials may have been, they did at least relieve us of the burden of convicting them ourselves. The 'small fry' were merely misled, submissively obeying strict orders; could one not justly see their misdeeds as having been committed under duress?" Too hastily perhaps, people arrived at these solutions, but everyone craved peace and quiet.

Recha, new problems still crop up in connection with these trials. For example, I sometimes ask myself if the precise illustration in the papers of instruments of torture and the detailed description of their use might not be poisoning the imagination of many a youth of our day. I am shocked by the apparent callousness with which young people listen in occasionally on the hearings. Quite frequently the judge has to call them to order as they sit there among the audience in shirt-sleeves, with legs crossed high, and chewing gum as if they were looking at a movie thriller.

But these too are merely regrettable side effects which certainly ought to be allayed but which are not sufficient reason, as I see it, to have the State abandon the serious attempt to account to itself for its past. To do this thoroughly is possible only by way of actual trial proceedings, which are hopeful action in themselves. It is to be hoped that the great care given to the jurisdiction and the very fact of its being open to the public might awaken and inform the younger generation, and that the facts which are brought to light by the testimony of the witnesses might penetrate the consciousness of the broad masses and become a warning. It is for this that the witnesses are bringing the sacrifice that is their testimony!

Today I must have you take a look into the courtroom. The dominant impression emanates from the presiding judge. To me, it is a great privilege to watch a man at work for whom the task of conducting a trial is indeed a heavy and burdensome responsibility; a man whose work is never routine; who looks to both sides—to accuser as to defense—who forbids any lack of discipline, any sidetracking into personal or political attack, and who leads back always onto the narrow path of truth. It is he, after all, who must assemble the mosaic from thousands of little stones and do it with minute care so as not to add, under any circumstance, a new wrong to the old. The witnesses often fall short in understanding this—and small wonder. To them, it is as if someone were pointing to one single grain of sand amid a desert full of suffered wrong, to have them say

21

whether that grain be brown or yellow. And if by any chance it turns out that years ago, at the pre-trials, they said that it was yellow, while now they call it brown, the defense rises triumphant; but in the witness, desperate wrath wells up and not infrequently brings on nervous collapse. Then it is vital that one of us—we now are four—should take the witness out, drive him to the hotel or to the Palm Gardens, and give him a chance to talk.

One of them said to me: "If I had had any idea that I would have to endure this kind of interrogation by the defense of my tormentor—as if I were the accused—I surely would never have come. In fact, I did not want to come at all; I was glad that I was finally forgetting; but then I felt I owed it to my dead comrades to speak about what we have suffered. If we keep silent now, all that suffering will have been in vain. Then, no one will ever learn from all that horror." And later on he added: "Believe me, I do not hate the German people altogether. Germans, too, suffered with us out there. And of course, there are in any country cynics, criminals, and sadists. But how to keep them from getting a free hand? . . ."

It reminded me of your last letter where you deplored with such despair how miserably the prosecution is conducted in your state of Mississippi against the murderers of the three men from CORE who had set out to work for civil rights, quite simply because the pertinent authorities are sympathetic to the murderers. And that in the Land of the Free! Such happenings can only force us all to our knees in a new kinship born from recognition of our own iniquity.

You asked also whether the Auschwitz survivors draw at least a pension from our government. But, of those who are living in countries of the Eastern bloc—and most of them are, of course, since they are by nationality Poles, Rumanians, Czechs, or Hungarians—neither the families of the dead nor the surviving victims of the horrible tortures receive any of the so-called "restitution payments" from the German Federal Republic. This is a result of the political circumstances of the post-war period. Nor are restitution payments made in East Germany.

Dear Recha,

Yesterday I discovered that the "Lilies of the Field" have actually "beat us to it." You don't know what I mean by that, because you probably have never heard the lovely story of the Protestant Sisters of Mary. But you ought to know it, because the very fact that such a thing is possible over here belongs with the image created by the miracle boom of Germany's economy.

During one of the heavy air raids over Darmstadt in the year 1944, a group of young girls and the teacher

25

of their Bible class made a vow that, should they survive that hell-fire night, they would live their lives henceforth purely in following the path of Jesus Christ. Such vows were made by many people, but these young women have lived up to theirs. Their story is full of "miracles," as have been those of all the great believers. I want to say only this much:

They wear a simple black dress and live together in a sort of evangelical convent which they have built with their own hands, under the guidance of a contractor. It includes a church, a guest house, a publishing and printing shop, and an old people's home. They also maintain in Jordan a house for ecumenical exchange, and in Jerusalem a vacation home for Jews who suffered under German National Socialism. They see as one of their main tasks calling upon the German people to repent and to ponder their guilt in the sin committed against Jews under the Third Reich. But what they themselves are doing may well be the most impressive proof of atonement to be found in Germany today. And of course these Sisters were also ahead of us in caring for the Auschwitz witnesses; for the trials have run since February, whereas we began only in May to show concern about the witnesses. The Sisters of Mary make it a practice to invite the Jewish witnesses to Darmstadt for a few days of recuperation, so as to spoil them a little in their Mother House with their selfless care.

For us, as I have said before, the Red Cross serves as patron, or you might say, as our "calling card." Yet, it is not a truly sterling card, for the German Red Cross was—as were the churches—the greatest disappointment of the prisoners. Only perfunctorily did it, or could it, seek admittance to them; and then it failed to shout into the world what monstrous horror was being meted out in the concentration camps; it did not, or could not, bring deliverance. On the contrary. It was by Red Cross ambulances that the poison gas was shipped which was to kill Jews by the hundred thousands. Perhaps one cannot hold the Red Cross administration responsible for this abuse. But it is these experiences the former inmates associate with the name of the Red Cross. This explains also why our letter is read by so many with such grave distrust; the letter in which we offer the witnesses our care and help, and which follows closely their official summons so as to reach them while still in their homeland; it is written under the letterhead of the Red Cross.

When we go to meet them then in Frankfurt, many of them are extremely reticent, until they sense that we are really sincere and do mean well by them. Then we are met by a gratitude which is both overwhelming and embarrassing. That we are able to obtain for them a decent pair of reading glasses, a hearing aid, or orthopedic shoes; that we help them through the teeming foreign city to get to the court cashier; that we invite them to our home to share a meal and see them back to the hotel afterward where they can take a rest, and from where they can always reach us if they need further help—all this makes them feel a little sheltered, which does them good.

How hard it is, nevertheless, to overcome their deep-seated mistrust; that is a thing I have experienced with one of our Poles. After two days of extreme reticence and caution he asked me, "Do you think that I could simply walk into a restaurant and order a meal?"

"Of course. Why not?"

"My wife has begged me not to; she is afraid I might be poisoned by a waiter whom someone would have bribed!"

"Oh, no, that most certainly won't happen; conditions in Germany are clear and clean again—the pestilence is over!"

"Really? But ever so many former criminals do run around free. Even some of those who are accused here. I have had to promise my wife not to testify against them. Even though they themselves may do me no harm, their friends well might. They say there is a powerful organization that aids former SS-men. For instance, do you by any chance know who helped that Zech-Nenntwich out of prison and right on all the way down to Cairo?"

No, I did not know. But I do know of the existence of the HIAG (Hilfe auf Gegenseitigkeit, i.e., Mutual Aid), a very affluent charity of the SS. I cannot judge to what extent this organization honestly helps people innocently involved, or whether it constitutes merely a kind of gang companionship. In any case, I managed to talk the Pole out of his fear that he might be persecuted here even today.

In the beginning, we also made mistakes in our first contacts with the witnesses. For instance: On the eve of his hearing, we had invited one of the Poles, together with three others, to the home of friends, so as to make a nice evening for them. Not to mention Auschwitz at all would have left them under the impression that we were not truly interested or did not really care. So the hostess asked them a few friendly questions, thinking that all of this might be of lasting value also to her grown-up children. The former prisoners began to talk; they went on and on and simply could not stop. As a result none of them slept that night in spite of sedatives, and one broke down the next day at the hearings. They saw, however, that we had meant well.

Ever since then we have been entertaining the witnesses only after the hearings are over. When the weather permits we go on walks with them, show them the town or whatever may interest them. And there is much variety in this. While some like to visit the Zoo, others say, "No thanks, of wild animals we have had enough . . ." Some ask to see the Goethe House and are much taken by the young student of Germanistic studies who is our guide and who talks about Goethe's childhood in a most lively way, and, to the amazement of witnesses from the Eastern bloc, completely without strewing in propaganda for democracy. Such astounding observations and remarks are like a window to another world. "How friendly all the clerks here are in serving the customer," one of them said after an employee of Opel had telephoned all around for half an hour, trying to locate somewhere the needed parts for his 1953 car. What the friendliness, trust, and gratitude on the part of the witnesses toward us really means is something one can grasp only if one realizes over and over again what they lived through in Auschwitz. There, at least two and a half million people were gassed, shot, or killed by injection; or they starved to death in stand-up cells, or died of typhus. Some sixty thousand have survived, a chance which was given primarily to doctors, medics, and linguists, who were useful as interpreters and scribes, or to indoor craftsmen, who were essential to the maintenance of the camp and its personnel. These were the "privileged." However, German nationals were always first to move up to such coveted positions.

Of the others, only the younger or the very healthy could survive, the adroit, the master-organizers, or those whose boundless strength of spirit sustained their body as well, no matter what might be inflicted upon it. I have no other way of explaining how a human being can survive, who is first beaten into unconsciousness; then forced to swallow a salt-drenched fish salad, which, as he vomits it, renewed beating forces him to eat again; and surviving that, he is suspended on a post with hands tied behind his back, for hours; nor does he die when he is placed in a stand-up cell, on a 30″ by 30″ floor, where only every third day is he given a bowl of watery soup.

For some reason, he is not to starve entirely to death, as do his neighbors in other stand-up cells whose agony lasts thirteen days. Recha! It takes you thirteen days to starve to death! The starving screamed with pain; one of them ate his shoes. I meant at first to spare you such atrocities since the newspapers are full of them in any case. But when you find yourself face to face with someone who lived through that and has survived, then you feel that you owe it to him to face what he endured instead of running from it, and yes, even to speak of it abroad.

And the man who lived through that was without hatred! You understand, don't you, how great a privilege it is to meet with such a man, and that allowed to be with him we are indeed the true recipients of a gift?

Dear Recha,

Even before the Auschwitz trials started, I knew
from books and secondhand reports a good deal of
what happened in the concentration camps. But
now, in meeting with the witnesses, I am aware
of a tremendous difference in whether one reads or
hears about such dreadful ordeals or whether one
stands face to face with people who have lived
through them.

Yesterday, I spent some hours with a man who as a
fifteen-year-old boy had come to Auschwitz with his

33

mother. From overcrowded cattle-cars they had jumped to the platform, terribly fatigued, thirsty, hungry, and dirty after the long days of the trip. Amid the chaos wrought by the ill-fated, milling crowd and under shouts of SS-men about them, the boy in some sort of relief reached for his mother's hand and whispered, "Look, Mother, over there, a Red Cross car; nothing much can happen to us here." Yet, in that very car lay stored the bottled poison gas! He was soon taken from his mother, and in that self-same night she suffocated in the gas chambers.

But Recha, more overwhelming even than the million figures is still the one voice of one man: the judge asked him, "Can you recall who stood there on the platform when you arrived in Auschwitz, and who was making the selections?"

The witness stares as from another world, and then he answers very softly, "No . . . I only looked about to see what was becoming of my wife . . . whom . . . they had . . . torn from my arms." Another one who never saw his love again.

Dear Recha, Night fell upon my writing yesterday; I had to interrupt. But now I want to tell about "my" three Rumanian women. They have just had a whole week's rest with the Sisters of Mary, and after that they spent another day with me. Can you imagine at all what it is like to have in your own home as guests people who were in Auschwitz?

They were a mother and a daughter and their friend, who had stood by each other closely at the camp. With great determination and intelligence it had been possible sometimes to do so. The mother is a doctor and an extraordinary woman. She is one of those who have survived by inner strength, through the physician's ethics. For instance, at a roll call a woman came in labor and was swaying with pain. The doctor noticed it and tried to hurry to her aid, but a whip quickly struck her in the face. The pregnant woman was led away, and no one ever saw her after that. Yet such a whiplash, for the attempt to be of help as a physician, brought on increased strength rather than defeat—a phenomenon proved by all else this woman lived to do.

Love for her child gave her the strength in all the forlorn misery of hunger, pain, exhaustion, to rise at midnight, when the shower room was empty, to awaken the dead-tired child so as to wash her thoroughly. Cleanliness meant preserving life.

These people are flickering still from inner tension with all these memories so freshly stirred. That is why I bedded them down, each in a different room, for a short siesta. Later, I found between the pillows most touching little notes of gratitude that they had scribbled on small bits of paper. But, gratitude for what? For just a little sympathetic understanding.

And such were the people who were to be crushed like vermin!

Dear Recha,

During these last few days, several women have been questioned who came from Israel, Rumania, and Florida. A scene came to be talked about in court, which I want to describe to you because it seems to me characteristic of the situation into which SS-men, and especially army officers and doctors, could chance when ordered to do "platform duty"; that is, to do the tagging for life or death immediately upon arrival of the trains. Several more "selections" were made still later in the camp, whenever it was necessary to "make room."

Imagine it if you can: a train rolls in, cattle cars packed to overflowing with perhaps a thousand luckless people. Of them, about two hundred and fifty men and women capable of doing work are to be sorted out; the others, some seven hundred and fifty, are shipped by truck straight to the lethal chambers. Baggage, of course, is taken from them right away and sent by prisoner detail to the "Canada barracks" —symbol of the wealthy land—there to be ransacked by SS-men for valuables that are then given to the SS, sent to the front, or left for winter welfare, depending on what there may be. Well, on that platform stand the doctors ordered to make decisions dealing out life and death. As the accused here, they all deny ever having done any platform duty whatsoever. But witnesses occasionally recognize one or another face, or a name which they heard at that time, a name they never did forget.

Thus also a witness from America. So gravely has she been impaired for life that even now she looks as if she had been freed from Auschwitz only just this moment. Before the hearing she turned to me and said, "Twenty long years I have been waiting for the day when this same name would come up before some court of law, the name of the murderer of my mother and all my beloved brothers and sisters, waited that I might testify at long last to the truth."

Rumor had had it in the cattle car that families would not be separated. Therefore, as the time came for them to step outside, the mother gave the two-year-old to her young daughter, then barely seventeen, and tied a scarf around her head to make her look a little older so she might be taken for the baby's mother. Then she herself picked up the three-year-old. The other children, four, seven, ten, and fourteen years of age, were standing by their side. But then the doctor, for whom she had been looking ever since, tore her small brother from her arms and threw him back at his mother, not caring that she could not catch him fast enough since she herself was carrying the three-year-old; the oldest sister he ordered to the able-bodied, the others all into the gas. Of course, that was not said; rather those tagged for death were invited, because of their fatigue, to ride up to the camp by car. The next day, when the sister was on kitchen duty and at the first opportunity asked about her family, the supervisor gave her the laconic answer, "They have long since gone up the chimney."

I am haunted by one basically senseless question: Did that doctor commit murder, or did he save from death? The order to send those seven hundred and fifty people into the gas had not been his; as best he could, he had tried to avoid this murder duty, but he could not hope to do so forever. Or was it that he saved the two hundred and fifty he found fit to work? One cannot in fairness ask this question, since aid or rescue had no part in it. I have described this scene to you nevertheless because it shows so very clearly the dilemma in which some SS-men could find themselves once they had yielded just one little finger to the devil.

I spent one whole day with this witness. She was gravely disturbed, ravaged by bitterness. But gradually and very gently I could try to point out the doctor's anguish, too. As he had stood before the court he had not shown the markings of brutality—though none of heroism either. As I was leaving her that night in the hotel she was in tears, and yet she was no longer quite so hard. At last, she took me lovingly into her arms and whispered,

"Maybe you are right."

Ruppertshain/Taunus
June 7, 1964

Dear Recha,

Many thanks for your warm understanding! One hears and reads so often that you over there are rather shocked by the mild sentences that our judges do pronounce over the former SS-men. You probably don't visualize what all a judge of our day, and over here, must take into account.

The other day during the hearing, a long treatise was read that dealt with the "suspended sense of wrong." It is distinguished from the "sense of right"—the feeling that one has acted legitimately—in this: that under different conditions, one would have been aware of doing wrong. The sense of wrong is "under certain circumstances" inactivated and turned off. You may recall that Shakespeare in his *Richard III* has the two murderers philosophize awhile before they kill the Duke of Clarence. For them too, it is a question of shedding this very sense of wrong. At first they claim that, after all, they have their "orders," and thus someone else will bear the guilt. They overcome their own bodily fear by calling on their manly vanity: "tall fellows" would they be, of whom the world would speak with some esteem. And the last vestige of their sense of wrong is pushed aside in glancing on the satchel full of gold that beckons as reward. To an ordinary weakling, these three factors—obedience to an order, misguided self-esteem, and personal advantage (in our case the prospect of a furlough, liquor, cigarets, increased sausage rations) may well suffice for him to commit murder. For the murder of millions, many another motive has to be added.

As one listens to the cases heard here in the Auschwitz trials, two other aspects enter in that may have played decisive roles in laying out the stage for the mass murders. Steeped in a hothouse atmosphere, the spirit shared by the guard personnel bred its own fever dreams in ghetto-like seclusion from the outside world. And demagogic cover-up embellished everything as service to some "ultimate ideal." From your last letter I conclude that you don't know the famous speech of Himmler to the SS-troops in which he put his own "Weltanschauung" in characteristic and impressive words, approximately in this way:

"There is no trick to ordering from one's desk a city cleared of Jews, but to follow through on that, to look upon a hundred or perhaps a thousand dead, upon ten thousand, a hundred thousand, women and children, too; to carry through on that and still remain a decent human being, that is where heroism has its true beginning!"

In this, that one could "still remain a decent human being," there is reflected the whole gamut of confusion which is, I think, so typically German. These "heros" then lived rather isolated lives in Auschwitz and in other concentration camps; heard there, if with variations, ever again the same familiar doctrine; and were dependent on each other in a kind of gangland loyalty. Under the threat that they themselves might be "sent up the chimney" should they give out information while on furlough, they adapted to this Himmler image of a "hero" in order to stay alive. For them, "remaining decent" meant giving candy to the children before they pierced their hearts with deadly hypos, or on soup line duty dishing double rations to those selected out (unless, as sometimes happened, they simply gave out nothing any more!). Telling the victims on the threshold of the lethal chambers that they would be given showers there was merely an expedient to prevent panic.

Though in this, too, there may have sounded a sad last remnant of a humane chord. For the SS-men lived in the belief that all of this just "had to be." Had they been totally perverted monsters, they would have lived in crime later on too, instead of turning to bookkeeping and nursing. A systematically preached "philosophy" seduced innumerable Germans and led them straight into the trap. Talk to a German of some life-philosophy and he will follow you up to the highest cliffs as well as down into the deepest pits! It is no accident that his word "Weltanschauung" does not exist in your American speech. Surely there are enough examples among all peoples of this earth to prove that revolutionary passions or war-time frenzy can whip men into committing deeds of inhumanity. But horribly new with our crimes was the very passionlessness of it all, the bureaucratic, cool, technically perfect mass annihilation.

In his *Maxims* Goethe has said: "Man as he acts is always without conscience; only he who looks on possesses one." But here, it was the onlooker himself who was the murderer, sheltered and calm behind his desk, not a seething people and their burning soul. This conflagration needed artificial fanning, race-hatred and "philosophy," to bring things up to all that fever pitch.

A Polish witness said to me with a haunting look of helplessness on his face: "You know what I can't ever get out of my mind? That actually the atmosphere in which such mass murders could be conceived, might with much greater likelihood be found among the Polish people than among the German. The Pole, with his national pride, his chauvinistic views, his antisemitism, his intolerance!" I said that I believe the decisive question is whether there is someone who will awaken evil passions or whether there is government that knows how to direct the forces bent on lawlessness and cruelty onto a better path with better goals.

All this is nothing new. Friedrich Theodor Vischer stated it long ago with great simplicity: "The art of government consists of laying responsibility into clean hands."

My Polish partner in this conversation is a patriot who puts all of his strength without reserve into helping his government attain what will be best for his own people. He said, "You can hear others, too, confess to this, with no one threatening to find them less than altogether true to the official line in thinking so." Whether he was right or not, objectively, I cannot judge. But to me it was of great importance

45

that I could feel true sincerity in what he said. Recha, I wish that thousands or even tens of thousands had the chance for such unprejudiced exchange of thought! How many scabs would fall from ancient wounds and let the clear new skin come through to light!

Over and over, when I talk to Germans about these SS-trials, they come up with the same trite, boring mention of atrocities committed by some other nations; they point to Dresden, to Hiroshima, and to the Russian Tscheka massacre, which are supposed to have cost thirty million lives among them. . . . I can only answer then as did one of my guests, a Rostock refugee, who lived in my home for two years: "All that may well be true; but I always say to myself simply that the dirt of others can never be the soap with which I cleanse myself."

The urge to lighten one's own pressing guilt by pointing to the guilt of others is very human, very natural. Yet, it will never move us forward; for it is nothing more than that!

Dear Recha,

Last night one of the witnesses told of a scene I would have liked to see come up in court. That it did not is not the judge's fault. He must, after all, restrict himself to hearing only such testimony as bears upon events charged here against these men who stand accused. He cannot probe deep into whatever else the witnesses might have to say about the Auschwitz camp. Otherwise the hearings would never cease. Yet, what this witness told me ought to be recorded:

A large number of women with small children are told to strip before the so-called "shower rooms"; one

47

mother, carrying a maybe one-year-old, until now gullible enough that she simply could not let herself believe the rumors that circulated about the camp, suddenly sees what is to happen. Gripped by despair, she throws herself down at the feet of a young guard imploring him to save at least her child. And she reminds him that he surely has wife and child himself and that he therefore must have mercy. What shall he do? He pushes her aside and shoves her forward with the others, across the threshold and inside. But at the moment when the doors are closing, screaming My Wife! My Child! he thrusts himself into the throng, and dies with them there in the gas.

Another witness told before the court that one SS-man had successfully slipped someone else out of the camp and tried to help him, too. But this time he was caught. Whereupon he, SS-man Pasteck, and the witness were chained together and led around the camp for all to see. "That caused amazement everywhere; no one had ever seen any such thing: an SS-man chain-coupled to a Jew!" He was savagely beaten and then shot. For three weeks afterward the Jew himself was "sharply questioned," which meant alternate torture and interrogation; they wanted to force from him details about the preparations for the flight. But in the end—no one knows why—he was not killed, but restored to his own work brigade. The result was that the other prisoners all lived in fear of him and shunned him because they thought that he had yielded something that was of use to the SS or else that he had been appointed to spy on them. Neither was true. How he survived at all no one can possibly explain. But ever since, he has been so beset by fear of persecution that he refused an interview to any paper whatsoever. With us, however, he gained confidence.

All witnesses agree that almost all SS-men have at one time or another, somewhere and to someone, shown signs of decency. Even the worst of brutes had "protégés." In the face of such facts, one comes upon questions of human values and relationships that concern all of us. Is it not as if even the most warped of human beings—perhaps one ought to say, an altogether alienated one—could not survive completely without love? Even an Eichmann and a Höss, they say, were "loving fathers."

Such thoughts stirred in the mind of a Rumanian teacher who had come here to testify and whom I took to visit a family up in the Taunus. She watched two youthful fathers in that family play with their children in a lovely way. "I wonder," she said as we drove back, "if you can understand; but all the time I tried to see those two young fathers in SS uniform and wondered whether they, too, would have been capable of beating and murdering human beings!"

Frankfurt/Main
June 21, 1964

Dear Recha,

All of this time, I have been telling you about the witnesses, the judge, and even the spectators; but it is the accused themselves who occupy my thoughts day and night. Oh Recha, it is torturous to see and hear them offer again and again their stereotyped denials of whatever it may be. And if a dozen witnesses agree in testifying that they saw with their own eyes how one or the other of these men picked out and beat or shot someone: No, that had not been he; there must be some mistake. Is it that such denial really serves a purpose for the accused? If I were a defense attorney, I would advise my client to admit the charge and then leave it up to me to clear him. As one of the accused, had I in the Third Reich made use of the State's licence accorded sadists, I would ask for the most severe of punishments or for a chance to expiate myself by doing some constructive penance, working perhaps lifelong and without pay in an orphanage or hospital so that I might gain back some peace of mind, if that would ever be possible. Obscuring guilt with such denials or passing it on to someone else, must needs cost the accused the always possible moment of grace. I myself find the attorney's manner of defense, as one can sense it even now, an ill service indeed to the accused. For the defender should here be minister as well.

The witnesses, who might have every right to bitterness and hatred, often defend those accused here a great deal better than they do themselves. One of them said to me the other day: "Why don't they have the backbone to confess to what they did, these heroes? Is not what they now say against their better judgment? All sin can be forgiven, all but the sin against the Holy Spirit!" For neither of us was there a need to probe into the meaning of the concept "sin against the Holy Spirit." I knew well what he meant and in that I agreed.

Once more I must return to what seems to me the most important question, raised ever anew in the minds of all concerned: What purpose does this trial truly serve? This question prevailed as well in various conversations held among us about the pros and cons—long since decided in the affirmative—of hearings to be held in Auschwitz proper. A Pole agreed: "The world will laud the earnestness of the attempt to sweep this filth out clean. Of course, the dead can't be revived, nor can the agonies be wiped away. The very thoroughness, however, of these trials, to which a local hearing would add that much more, will mean a cleansing for the German State. Only into a cleaned-up house can one invite a guest."

I asked him in return: "By 'cleansing,' do you mean the trial as a whole or just the local hearing as now planned?"

To which he replied, "The trial as such is a first step; the local hearing a second; but more important still will be the third: the thoughtfulness the trials must engender, the questioning and probing—when and where were the rails so wrongly shunted as to let an Auschwitz come about at all? This is the question that all nations of this world must ask themselves."

In contrast to such positive evaluation of the trials, there is the skeptical view, the objection, with which I met equally often. A most appealing, intelligent, and surely decent young merchant said to me: "Is it

not terrible, this German thoroughness of ours? First
we murder and kill with technical precision and then
we spread out all that dirt for the whole world to see!
Would anyone else do such a thing?"

But I replied: "I don't consider it spreading out
dirt. I see the trials rather as analysis, a true cathar-
sis, performed by a conscientious doctor whose di-
agnosis may well be of use not merely for the patient
now concerned but for all who might be prone to
the same illness."

It was a joy to see how he reacted to my answer. And
yet, his sense of helplessness remained. "Just look at
Russia," he said. "Twenty or thirty million Russians,
supposedly, were slaughtered in the Stalin purge;
how could he find so much assistance in that intrinsi-
cally friendly land? Then Khrushschev came and had
Stalin declared a criminal (though he had been his
faithful follower for years); and all that had happened was just pushed aside. The book is closed. The
world accepts it, just like that! One merely shrugs
and says, 'That's Asia for you!' "

I don't know what your answer would have been.
But I tried also to make clear to him that in compari-
son with such dictatorial finality, it signifies consider-
able progress that here the possibility exists for
public trials of this kind, and that this very fact
constitutes hope.

But now toward the end, I want to tell you of yet one more very moving moment that I had this week. It was a sunny summer afternoon, and I was walking in the Taunus with two Poles who had survived the Auschwitz hell and who, here in the forest air, were making the attempt to cleanse themselves of all the stirred-up recollections. We passed a garden where two little children were engrossed in playing in a sandbox, baking sand cakes and decorating them with tiny daisies that they had eagerly picked in the meadow. Enchanted, pensive, the two Poles stood still to watch. "Only a playing child or a bird in flight can still my tears," I quoted Justinus Kerner. After a thoughtful silence, one of them said: "Indeed —and still, it always makes me cry to see a child at play. Because I will always see beyond it those who were playing back in Auschwitz. That God should have stood mute when they were killed—I can no longer have faith that there is a God . . ."

I had to think of the pages in Primo Levi's book*
where he describes how, after a selection had been made, but was not carried out until two days later, he had watched from his bunk the old, deeply de-vout Jew Kuhn as he donned his little prayer cap and, swaying back and forth, gave his fervent thanks unto the Lord that he had not been sent off to his death that day. Levi continues then with his own

---

* Primo Levi, *Ist das ein Mensch?* S. Fischer Verlag.

thoughts: "Has the old Kuhn gone altogether out of his mind? Does he not see the young Greek over there, who can only stare into the light, no longer capable of any real thought, because he knows that two days hence he is to go into the gas? Does the old Kuhn not know that his turn will be next? If I were God, I'd spit Kuhn's prayer right back down onto the ground!"

It turned my thoughts to the Old Testament and to the Psalms that are so full of passionate quarrel against God. Preoccupied by all this thought, I stood there at the fence next to the Pole who had sunk ever deeper into sorrow. "And yet," I finally could say, "you were the one who asked to swear 'by God Almighty' instead of by the civil formula."

"Oh yes, indeed, I wanted to; and not just as a matter of tradition. I'll always want to, in things like this . . . I can't rightly tell you why . . ."

Here stood a man who had struck me as the reproach personified against the age-old concept of our God; yet, he had gained at the same time that faith which —as is written in the Law—does not make graven images of Him. I don't know if you understand what moved me so: he had retained within himself a simple clarity—no longer that of a small child—but the mature naïveté of a man who has gone through and past all doubt up to the threshold of despair; one who has weighed every theory and argument by the integrity of his own mind and reached the limit of endurance. But at the brink of the abyss a voice has overtaken him: "Where were you when I made the Earth?" Within himself he had resolved the contradiction: there is no God; but neither is there not a God. He had resolved it not by intellect, but by the way he lived.

Once more we came to talk about the children who were so concentrated on their game that they had not noticed us at all. "I wonder why Jesus so loved to have children about?" the Pole asked out of his deep thought. "He knew of the abyss that is the human heart; perhaps he, too, found comfort in the little ones."

And at that very moment, the four-year-old got up and stuck a little flower through the fence into the hand of the sad man: "Here . . . that's for you!"

Frankfurt/Main
June 28, 1964

Dearest Recha,

I wrote to you the other day that I am haunted day
and night by thoughts connected with the trial. And
I did not exaggerate. Only by this, in any case, can I
explain the dream I had last night, so clear, so vivid,
so intense, that I can tell it here, in every detail.

I saw the whole stage of the courtroom, the accused
and the defense, the prosecutor and additional plain-
tiffs, and in the middle the three judges; Hofmeyer,
the presiding judge, in the center, the jury to both
sides. All stood. The judge read the sentences. Ac-
quittal . . . two years . . . five years . . . ten years . . .

life. Then his image grew larger and larger, his voice louder and louder, the audience swelled to thousands upon thousands, and he continued: "And now, beyond these judgments so pronounced, I sentence all those here who were of age in 1933—and I include myself—to be confined for life in moral prison; for each of us has helped, be it by blindness or inadequate resistance, to bring about conditions such as have made criminals of all these weaklings. What happened in our time can neither be undone nor atoned in punishment!"

Recha, that it was possible to have an Auschwitz within so civilized a population, where 95 percent were baptized Christians—this very fact will not allow us ever to sit back and rest until we have found where and when the rails were shunted wrong; and even, where and when I shunted mine in the wrong way.

In this, I see the true sense of these trials.

It has been a great help to me that during all this time I could be in close contact with you. Let me thank you for that once more, dear Recha.

The Little Town of Auschwitz (Oswiecim)

lies in Poland, between Krakow and Kattowitz, in swamp terrain where the supply of drinking water is extremely poor.

In 1940, the concentration camp was established there with thirty Germans, professional criminals all, as "Capos," i.e., guards.

In the beginning, nearly all the prisoners were Poles. Surrounding villages were all evacuated, not only so as to isolate those held as prisoners, but also because the gassing and the mass cremations that were carried out there did literally smell to heaven.

The camp, constantly enlarged, held later an average of 100,000 prisoners.

In that camp alone, at least two and one half million were gassed, beaten or shot to death, killed by injection, or else starved to death in stand-up cells.

Approximately 60,000 have survived.

In Germany proper, there were twenty-five concentration camps, each with its network of out-lying camps, thus altogether several hundred.